Flight of the Midgie!

STORIES OF SCOTLAND'S TINIEST BITING BEASTIES

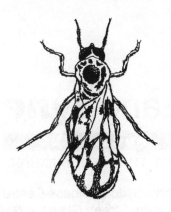

Lang**Syne**

PUBLISHING

WRITING *to* REMEMBER

Publisher's note

The publishers are grateful for the invaluable assistance given by Mr Eric Allison, Founder and Organiser of the Stirling Midgie Festival Competition, who gave permission for selected entries to be reproduced here.

We would also like to thank the *Scotsman Publications*, Edinburgh, for permission to reproduce the article by Albert Morris, and to the *Scots Magazine*, who first published the story *A Fine Summer's Evening*.

Stirling Midgie Festival winning entries © Eric Allison 1990.

Lang**Syne**
PUBLISHING
WRITING *to* REMEMBER

Strathclyde Business Centre
120 Carstairs Street, Glasgow G40 4JD
Tel: 0141 554 9944 Fax: 0141 554 9955
E-mail: info@scottish-memories.co.uk

First Published 1990. Reprinted 1995, 2003 and 2007.

Printed By Thomson Litho, East Kilbride
Design and artwork by Roy Boyd and David Braysher
© Lang Syne Publishers Ltd 2003
ISBN 1-85217-116-2

Flight of the Midgie!

STORIES OF SCOTLAND'S TINIEST BITING BEASTIES

contents

Introduction

The female is deadlier than the male. Human blood is her favourite food
and she attacks with deadly precision. She is no respecter of persons, the
Duke of Edinburgh having been among thousands of recent victims.
During the Second World War Scottish soldiers, training in the
Highlands, branded her a worse enemy than Hitler. Lotions and
potions, camouflage clothing and smoke clouds are just some of the
clever tactics we humans employ to dodge her unwelcome attentions.

Her proper name is *Culicoides impunctatus* which you may not have
heard before. But you will know her everyday name — the MIDGIE!

Never in the field of human conflict has so much pain been inflict-
ed on so many by one so tiny!

There are actually 34 different species of midge flying around
Scotland. Five attack people but at least 85% of ALL attacks on humans in
Scotland are made by the *Culicoides impunctatus*.

In these pages we present an entertaining and informative mixture
of stories, facts, poems and illustrations all about these tiny biting beasties.

Journalist Albert Morris says: "Of all the insects that have raised
bumps and itchy spots on me and drawn blood from my cringing skin, I suppose the Highland midge has caused me the greatest melancholy."

Eunice Wyles challenges the theory that all life forms evolved from
a single cell, at least as far as midgies are concerned. They flew straight out
of Hell, according to her highly original poem!

We have the true story of a Scottish family who found themselves
wandering the streets of a strange town in the small hours dressed in pyjamas, having survived a midgie attack "bloodied and muddied from the
biggest battle of our lives". Another real-life story tells how the little
blighters can kill romance stone dead.

And there are amusing fictional tales. One tells how a midgie turned
a night at the opera into absolute chaos. Another tells of a young camping
couple who couldn't understand why their host was so anxious to fill his
empty tobacco pouch!

*If you've been a victim, or are about to become one, this
book is dedicated to you. To boldly go where the midgie lies in wait proves
that you've got guts and stamina — as well as being an absolute glutton for
punishment!*

Twenty things you'll want to know about the Midgie

No. 1 The midge is a relative of the mosquito. When we breathe out they home in, attracted by the carbon dioxide in our exhaled breath. They stick their hollow, needle-like noses into the tissues below the skin and suck up our fluids and blood. There seems to be little doubt that humans are their favourite grub!

No. 2 The female midge's mouthparts are like hypodermic syringes and she works by rasping, rather than piercing the skin. We are not alone in being their targets for blood meals. Horses and cows are just as liable to find themselves under attack. So too are caterpillars, moths, butterflies and dragonflies.

No. 3 The midge starts life as an egg. After hatching the tiny worm-like larva spends 10 months in an effective non-feeding state before starting to develop. The process to arrival at adulthood is completed within a few days.

No. 4 Midges need human blood to develop their eggs. But the very first batch of eggs can be produced without this, using energy stored when the female was at the non-feeding stage of her development. As many as 80 eggs can be produced in this way, thus showing how the midgie population can keep on expanding even without involuntary human donors!

No. 5 A priority of the female after the first eggs are laid is to go out in search of her initial blood meal. The male midge gets his sustenance from nectar and other plant juices — he is most strictly a vegetarian!

No. 6 The mating game is played when his antennae detect the high-pitched vibrations of the female's wing-beats. Later she will lay her eggs on mud or wet soil.

No. 7 The midgie arrives as a tiny worm-like form in late summer and develops over winter to become a fully fledged flying mini-monster just in time for the height of the next tourist season in Scotland!

No. 8 Scotland is the worst affected country in the world from midgies. Apart from the winter months, only April and May are midge-free. The west and north are their favourite hunting grounds where the boggy and acidic ground provides ideal conditions for breeding. Midgies are not usually found on higher ground, above 500 metres, as the wind curtails their ability to fly.

No. 9 The Highland midgie is in the order *Diptera*, which is the scientific classification for flies with two wings. Its body weight is about half a microgram and its wingspan is 1.4mm.

No. 10 The origin of the midgies can be traced back 60 million years, but around 200 years ago they were in short supply in the Highlands, possibly due to cyclical factors in the midge population. Famous travel writers like Boswell and Johnson, Wordsworth or Pennant do not make any mention of the scourge. Gaelic proverbs allude to the midgie's presence, however, but not their bite.

No. 11 But one report from this period certainly makes mention of the menace. After the failure of the Jacobite Rebellion in 1746 Bonnie Prince Charlie was a fugitive, hunted in the heather by English redcoats... and the midgie. John O'Sullivan, a fellow fugitive, wrote: "The Prince was in a terrible condition, his legs and thy's cut all over from the bryers: the mitches and flys wch are terrible in yt country, devoured him, and made him scratch those scarfs, wch made him appear is he was cover'd with ulcers."

No. 12 Cousins of *culicoides impunctatus* include *culicoides halophilus*, *culicoides nubeculosis* and *culicoides obsoletus* - hal, nub and ob for short! Hal likes the salt marshes of the Scottish coast. Neb loves farm stables, feeding on cattle, though she's not averse to some human blood. Ob frequents lowland towns and although her bite is less ferocious she is more persistent, making quite a nuisance of herself in parks and on golf courses, especially during wet summers.

No. 13 Midgies are particularly problematic because they swoop in thick black clouds - a black rain cloud is bad but a midgie swarm is quite something else! Concentrations of larvae have been known to reach 10 million per acre.

No. 14 Midgies like the twilight and are at their most dangerous around dawn and dusk. The sun is their enemy - they will never be out in the midday sun, but if the weather is dull and overcast they can strike at any time.

No. 15 The midgie has a highly developed sense of smell which it uses to detect the presence of several chemicals in the body odour of humans and other animals.

No. 16 A survey of 2,000 people discovered that one in four used herbal-based repellents. Oil from the neem tree is particularly effective.

No. 17 Different name tags are applied to the various types of midgies. No-see-ums is a common name in North America, and in Norway they are known as knotts. The Gaelic word is meanbh-chuileag, meaning tiny fly.

No. 18 Bites can range from being a persistant irritant to causing large, painful and unsightly sores.

No. 19 The midge is blamed for the under-population of the Highlands and the cheaper land prices there. Forestry workers can lose an average of one day's work a week because of acute midgie attacks.

No. 20 But the little blighters' days could be numbered. American scientists are making considerable advances on new, more effective repellents. And climatic changes, including the warming effect and decreased rainfall, could lead to their favourite breeding grounds drying up.

Oh, Midge O' Scotland!

by Elspeth Beaton

A wee boy took a midgie hame;
it wisna' very fat.
He fed it on some lamb chops
an' peas, an' chips, an' that.

He spoke tae it in Gaelic:
it seemed tae unerstan'.
Its mither cam' frae Skye, ye see;
its faither frae Oban.

It grew intae a hulkin' thing,
wi' jaws an' teeth tae match.
But sudden-like it flew awa'.
It had some eggs tae hatch.

It drapped them doon on Rothesay
an' mair eggs on Dunoon.
It sprayed a few on Millport,
an' lots on Largs an' Troon.

Then northward it did travel
till oot o' eggs it ran,
an' so it gi'ed tae Scotland
Deterrent Number Wan!

Close encounters of the midge kind!

by Wilma Davidson

Why, you might wonder, were my husband and I, with Siamese Cat on a lead, wandering around the streets of a Scottish town in our pyjamas at four o'clock in the morning? I hasten to add that the pyjamas were worn on top of T-shirts and shorts, or does that make matters worse?

We might have emerged from this predicament with some dignity had the local population all been tucked up in bed, but we had the misfortune to meet the only other imsomniacs in Lairg that night — a couple taking their sick dog to a vet, who, I'm sure, would be pleased to see them at that hour! I should add that they were civil and apparently understanding of our explanations — or perhaps just being polite.

I must admit that, in spite of our claim to be quite average people, the presence of our Siamese cat on camping trips was quite usual. He was well used to camping, but his appearances on these occasions did raise a few eyebrows and was entirely the cause of our problems.

We had left Ullapool the previous evening to look for a camp site, pitch our tent for the night, and continue on our way to Scrabster and the Stromness ferry in the morning. We found the camp site without any difficulty — but the driver forgot to stop. I told him it was the last one for umpteen miles.

"Nonsense", he declared, "there must be another one before that!" So on he drove. We soon found ourselves in bleak moorland. After a while he stopped. It was getting dark.

"Let's just stop here", he said. "Not here for heaven's sake", I said. A tent I can thole but I do like what are politely termed 'amenities'. However, he was determined. There was no persuading him to turn back to the previous camp site which he declared was "closed for the night anyway".

"They don't close", I muttered in despair but he was already unloading the tent.

So I took Siamese for a walk while our Pioneer pitched the tent, unrolled sleeping bags, inflated lilos and prepared a hot water bottle for the comfort of One Cat and His Mum.

We settled down just before it got really dark. We managed to get some sleep in spite of the all-too-close munching of the sheep which can be quite frightening when you can't see them.

I woke about two in the morning thinking that it wasn't too bad a place to spend the night after all. The sight of other tents had reassured us. We were warm and it wasn't raining or even windy. Little did we know...

I then realised what had wakened us. Siamese was clawing at the door. Siamese wanted OUT. Siamese wanted to spend a penny or whatever cats spend on such occasions. Now if I explain that Siamese slept in tent with collar and lead tied to Father's knee (oh dear!) you can understand how easily he had managed to waken us. One frantic dive towards the door, Man hauled between tent-pole and cat-on-lead, one leg suspended in mid-air... OK, we then made the fatal error, but what else could we do? We opened the flap of the tent a teensie-weensie bit, just Siamese-cat-sized, and out trotted one desperate cat to answer nature's call.

He soon squirmed back in again looking much relieved, settled down and — scratched his ear. Then the claws went to his neck, his rump, then his ear again. He rubbed his eye. Then his other eye. Then I felt an itch. Then another. Pioneer was scratching too. Cat by this time was going wild. They had come in on his coat and they had found us too. Thousands of them. Midges. Of course.

Within minutes Cat was in awful distress. We rubbed him with towels and clawed at ourselves but it was soon plain that we were fighting a losing battle. We could see a steady stream of them pouring through the inch-square hole in the doorway. They were soon squeezing in through every minute space in the zips and fabric of the tent, hungry for blood. We must have murdered thousands, but there seemed to be millions more. Our hands and faces were black with them. Cat was squealing and shrieking like a berserker.

After a desperate half hour we decided to abandon ship. We got dressed in T-shirts and shorts and prepared to throw everything into the car, anywhere, any way. But changing our clothes was the worst thing we could do — they had all the more skin to attack. And they didn't half take advantage. So we decided to put our pyjamas back on top of our clothes to lessen the area of attack.

We fled to the car, threw everything in, tent, bedding, luggage, Cat, all in a heap, and headed off into the night with the greatest acceleration our Fiesta has ever achieved. The windscreen was black with them. Visibility was nil. They were piled an inch thick round the car. Every flick of the wiper blades cost an army of fatalities. They were now inside the car and still attacking in droves. Windows open, air vents open, driver yelling above the engine roar, Cat yowling like a banshee...

Gradually, after many miles, the onslaught began to subside. Bedraggled, bloodied, exhausted and defeated, we crawled into Lairg and slowly cruised around the town looking for some way to help our situation.

We found the loo. After a quick reconnaissance we discovered it was open and the good citizens of the town were nowhere to be seen. So, feeling like a vagabond, guilt-ridden by my appearance, bloodied and muddied from the battle, I sneaked into the wee white house for a wash and change of clothes. All seemed to go well till I got back to the car to discover pyjama-clad husband holding Siamese-on-lead deep in embarrassed conversation with two normal humans. At least they were laughing. They listened politely. They admired our scars. And they didn't call the police.

The incident described is absolutely true and the Davidsons haven't camped on moorland since! A relative of the family was attacked by midges in the garden of their Helensburgh home. She had spent a month on holiday in Borneo, but the 'giants' who attacked, leaving her like a measles victim, were far worse than anything encountered in the jungle!

Midgies on the Moss

by Ann Richard

Ae summer's day while castin' peat a cloud cam ower the moss,
The rain began ti fa' and as Ah pleitered through the dross
 A host o' midgies bent on blood cam fleein' ower the hill;
Ti hae a feast upon ma flesh wis certainly their will.
Doon went ma spade an' aff Ah ran as fest as Ah could ging,
They blotted oot ma vision, Ah could scarcely see a thing
As ower the heather clumps Ah louped ti find ma freedom rare;
Ti hae them sook awa' at me, the thocht Ah couldna bear.
They landed on ma heid, ma face and baith ma hands as weel,
Ah wisna gaen ti be the host for sic a tasty meal.
Ah threw ma coat aroond my heid an' lichted up ma pipe,
But michty me the chokin' reek was far waur than the bite.

Don't lose yer heid

On Stirling Bridge, attacked by a midgie,
Bold Rob Roy cried, "Fight me! Wid ye?
Ye'll no beat me, ye deil wi' wings,
I'm no feart o' yer bites and stings!"

Roond his heid he slashed wi' fury,
Missed the midge — cut off his toorie.
Frustrated anger made him shiver,
Headlong fell into the river.

So if a midge, it gets yer goat,
And temper rumbles in yer throat,
Remember Rob and calm ye doon
Or ye'll lose yer heid or maybe droon.

"Nastier than Hitler"

The London *Times* disclosed that clouds of tiny midges, which populate the west of Scotland from summer to early autumn, and send grown men running for cover, are costing the economy millions of pounds a year.

The top people's paper reported that "swarms of the mosquito-like creatures, smaller than the top of a pinhead, are posing a threat to Scotland's tourist industry."

And an Aviemore conference was told they are the scourge of farmers and forestry workers because of their voracious appetite for human blood.

Rosemary Long told, in the Glasgow *Evening Times*, how the first real organised attack on midgies came during the Second World War. "Troops manning gun sites in remote crannies on the West Coast voted the midge nastier than Hitler," according to Rosemary.

"The powers-that-be were forced to take steps to develop some kind of protection... otherwise it is doubtful whether we'd have won the war."

Locals and visitors to Loch Lomond were delighted by an 'invasion' of pied flycatchers. A record number of the rare birds, which had come all the way from Africa, was reported at Inversnaid reserve.

The Royal Society for the Protection of Birds told the *Evening Times*: "With the swarms of midges around at the moment, which flycatchers eat, the more 'pied flys' the better!"

They flew oot o' Hell's open windae!

by Eunice Wyles

See Darwin's "ORIGIN OF SPECIES",
an' a' the claims based on his thesis
that, "ALL LIFE EVOLVED FROM A SINGLE CELL"...
'sno true! for midgies flew straight oot o' Hell!

The story goes... yin month o' June
mair souls were gauin up than doon,
causin' depression a' ower Hades,
whaur, on balance, men ootnumber ladies!

So, efter a heavy nicht o' Sin
Auld Nick wis enjoyin' a long lie-in,
He pu'ed his duvet up ower his heid,
tae droon-oot the piercin' screams o' the Deid...

The nicht-shift, caked wi' furnace grime,
wir gettin' their jaickets at lousin'-time,
"The Fire's gauin' oot!" a stoker cries,
"Ye're needin' tae bring doon mair supplies"...

"Don't", snapped Nick, "gie me yer worries,
just chuck on that pile o' missionaries —
Ah ken they're gey green an' fu' o' sap,
but they'll dae the noo, while Ah tak' ma nap!"

Wi' that, he scratched an' turned richt ower,
tae forget Hellfire for half-an-hour...
(it crossed his mind that Central Heatin'
micht stop a' this infernal greetin'...

He should've kep thae Sales Reps back,
an' burnt them **efter** he'd heard their crack!)
Meanwhile, the fire began tae smeek,
an' shin a' Hell wis fu' o' reek...

"Open a windie, quick!" says he,
"that lum'll be the daith o' me!"
but chokin' fumes spread thick an' fast —
(Damnation's Fires forever last)...

Auld Satan spat, an' coughed, an' cursed,
an thocht his lungs wir fit tae burst ....
while afore his een, his past wis reelin',
some gallus midgies crossed the ceilin'...

Too late! he minded the windie gapin',
an' couldnae stop them fae escapin'...
Oot they bizzed, an' felt the air
draw them up through the atmosphere,
an' land them on a marshy dell
in Scotland — the nearest land tae Hell!
there, tae multiply an' thrive
by eatin' a'body alive.

Doon the ages, Scots hae tried
new weys tae commit mass-midgicide —
but, quicker waitin' for Hell tae freeze!
best tae mak' a fire wi' green sap trees,
for midgies are drawn tae heat, an watter,
but smeeky reek shin mak's them scatter —
they ken that whaur there's smoke there's flame,
an' Auld Nick micht come an' tak' them hame!

Opera fiasco on the shores of Loch Fiddel

by Stewart Craig

It was in all the newspapers — "Alma Pavaritti to sing on the shores of Loch Fiddel". The town of Glen Fiddel had been a buzzing hive since the world famous opera singer had announced her intention to perform a concert by the lochside.

"Whit way does she want tae come here?" asked old Calum of the grocer Hugh Pugh. The shopkeeper had looked contemptuously down his thin nose at the shame of Glen Fiddel. Calum McDougal lived rough in a shack beside the loch, had shaved twice in his sixty nine years and when drunk, which was often, looked more like a rabid English sheepdog than a man.

"If you want to know", sneered Pugh, adjusting his specs and handing Calum's wine over the counter, "Alma Pavaritti claims ancestral links with this town and a need to discover her roots here." "Ancestral links!" scoffed Calum, "her grandfaither ran a chip shop back in the twenties, an' if her voice is anything like his chips, we'll need plenty of sauce to go wi' it!"

That night there was a meeting held in the back room of the local pub 'The Pop Inn', run by its proprietor, Murphy the bald ex-prize fighter. Murphy had not changed the name of the pub despite the fears of the local priest, Father Hannigan, that a repercussion of last year's events might occur when some persons unknown had added the letters "es" at the end of Pop and the pub had been inundated by newly converted Japanese tourists seeking an audience with His Holiness.

They would not be discouraged, and eventually for the sake of peace and quiet, Murphy had blessed the gathering and sent them forth, but not before he had sold them all a miniature of Bell's whisky each in the guise of Holy water.

At the meeting sat all the influential people of Glen Fiddel's community: Murphy, Pugh the grocer, Father Flannigan, the builder and Councillor Kelly, McGill the local PC, and last but not least, McPherson the farmer on whose land the event would take place.

"It's a momentous moment in the history of Glen Fiddel," said Pugh.

"A great honour for the spirit of our people," added Father Flannigan.

"It's going to mean a great deal of money for us all," cut in McPherson, "think, all of you, what it will mean. All those fans all that cash, think!"

Pugh saw a chain of grocers across the land, McGill saw himself Chief Inspector, Kelly saw a peerage, Father Flannigan, always more vain, a sainthood. Murphy dreamt of sun and sex, whilst the quiet McPherson saw power beyond his dreams at his fingertips.

"Listen, boys", he said, "it's a chance in a million, if we can put up the cash we can make a bundle."

"How do you get that kind of money?" asked PC McGill.

"Our business and property is our collateral," answered McPherson, "Councillor Kelly has a plan."

"Our estimates will be away above what it will cost", said Kelly, "believe me we can do it cheap and make a killing." Kelly brought out the plans of the staging and seating plus the pricing.

"Bloody hell!" said Murphy, seeing the costs, "I know she's a big girl but what's the stage to be made of, steel girders?"

McPherson interrupted, "We all have something to contribute here tonight," he said, "with Kelly, Murphy and myself, it's money, with PC McGill it's co-operation and a blind eye, with you Father Flannigan it's your blessing and a promise to keep your nose out."

"I'd like the church to share in this venture," said the priest quietly, having remembered the thousands of pounds in the steeple fund, "I'll contribute financially, I have a bit put by."

That night Glen Fiddel Enterprises was born and they all signed the contract. Now the discussion turned to other problems such as accommodation. How was the small town going to cope with the thousands of fans that would descend? Where would they stay? Bed & Breakfast notices were springing up like the dead on resurrection day. Farmer Ritchie had been quizzed by Councillor Kelly about his ad in the paper for unlimited beds at the piggery.

"Well, it's like this", Ritchie had confided, "I've converted one of the pig sheds, forty two bunks I've pit in there."

"Don't you think that provides a health hazard?" Kelly had asked.

"Naw, naw, silly", replied Ritchie, "dinnae be daft, I'll be alright, I'll no be sleepin' with them, I'll be in the hoose."

Kelly had shaken his head and given up. "What about Calum?" asked Pugh slyly, "his shack is where the stage is going to be."

"He'll have to go", they all replied in unison.

"But he has nowhere else to stay but the Loch," reminded Father Flannigan.

"Then what does God say?" demanded McPherson. They all looked to the priest who sat in silent prayer, listened to his conscience, ignored it as usual and said, "God says burn the shack!"

The meeting ended and by noon the next day, Calum was evicted and his shack burning. PC McGill and the rest presided over the operation whilst Calum, his heart breaking, stood in silence with head held high and shoulders back.

Alma arrived! The streets of Glen Fiddel were festooned with banners strung from lamp-post to lamp-post proclaiming her fame and skill. Crowds cheered as the limousine cruised slowly past through the showers of confetti and paper streamers The councillors overcame the initial shock of the lipsticked whale dressed in curtains as it emerged gradually from the vehicle.

"It's like a dinghy inflating," thought PC McGill as he watched Alma appear bit by bit through the seemingly impossibly small door.

"Good God!" mumbled Pugh as his hand disappeared into the dough of her diamond studded paw.

"Darrrlingss " purred Alma, planking great sink plunger kisses on the mouths of the local dignitaries, the savagery with which she withdrew her kiss from McGill causing his top set of false teeth to be sucked free and smash on the pavement.

"My..a..grandpapa's home!" she cried, throwing her great arms wide. The crowds cheered and followed as the star lumbered daintily up the main street.

"This is where your grandfaither had his shop", said Kelly proudly, stopping before the Chinese takeaway. Silence and drama filled the air. Alma like a silent screen goddess mimed her emotions, her large lips trembled with controlled emotion, "She's like somethin' ye'd see in the films", whispered PC McGill. "Aye," agreed Pugh, "Moby Dick!"

The star's inward emotions were given life as she silently portrayed memory, love, pain, and each mime brought a gasp from the crowd. A lump of tear hung on her false eyelashes, a ham of a forearm rested across her brow as she assumed the stance of unendurable loss.

"Ah wis sick where you're standin!" The crowd gasped in disbelief. Calum stood forward, "Aye, twice, an' it wis your grandfaither's rotten white puddens that did it tae", he shouted, pointing an accusing finger.

Alma gasped at the insult and the tear was sucked back. "Remove this creature from my sight!" she spat.

Loch Fiddel had never seen the like. Kelly's men had done their task well. Over a thousand people sat in the benches that surrounded the stage. An orchestra of fifty musicians tuned their instruments. On the loch, moorhens swam to the melodies of violins whilst the far off cliffs echoed with kettle drums. The stage was set, dusk was falling and spotlights lit the scene.

Alma appeared. Applause filled the twilight as her elephantine form swept majestically across the sagging boards. Her dress fluttered in the breeze and would have been the envy of any passing ship short of a mainsail. The conductor poised, his baton high; then struck. The strings, woodwinds and percussions thundered an introduction, starlings flew in flocks overhead. Alma's hands gripped before her, she stared at the heavens, her face a painting of piety as if listening to inspired words. The music calmed, became a wave, became a ripple; she sang!

Her voice rose softly from the caverns of that great body and was controlled to perfection, rising higher and higher; it blessed the loch with its beauty and Calum, from his perch in a tree, listened intently.

The midge had come attracted by the myriad floodlights but as he danced before them a strange vibration took hold of his tiny soul. He flew twisting and turning in its beguiling beauty and followed the source of this mystical reverberation that brought back memories of his time as a chrysalis. The insect's senses were lost in a sea of feeling, onward he flew willingly towards the heavenly inspiration, to the birth of his creation, right down Alma's throat.

The singer stopped abruptly! Her hand flew to her mouth; to her throat. The music faltered; stopped. Alma choked, gave a deafening belch through the microphone, then fell back. There was an almighty crash and a splintering of wood, a cloud of dust obscured the stage. The crowd gasped and rose to its feet as the dust rolled aside revealing a great gaping hole where the star had once been.

"Oh my God," prayed Father Flannigan.

"Bloody Hell," wept Kelly.

"She'll sue!" cried McPherson.

PC McGill's jaw went slack, his bottom set of teeth crashed to the ground.

"Ha! Ha!", laughed Calum.

With winches and block and tackle Alma had been recovered from the hole. It seemed she was unconscious and Pugh being the only one to possess a first aid certificate had administered mouth to mouth resuscitation, his bravery being admired by all.

The dust encrusted star had come round and looked up into the eyes of her saviour. A strange expression had gilded her face, causing the eyes to soften and Pugh's hair to hackle. Whether it was love or concussion we will never know, but no action was taken against Pugh; but for the rest her rage was insatiable. Kelly was imprisoned, Murphy and McPherson ruined, Father Flannigan excommunicated and PC McGill driven from the force.

Within the month Alma and Pugh were wed. Alma, bedecked in a tent of white and pearl, had squeezed down the aisle towards her beloved saviour Pugh, who stood supported in a valium and whisky trance with the look of a drowning man on his face. All of Glen Fiddel agreed that the rest had got off lightly.

As for Calum? He rebuilt his home, the stage and seating providing enough for a shack twice the size of his old one, and plenty of timber left for an extension.

And the midge? Well, if it's true and we are what we eat, then at this moment the midge is at Covent Garden singing '*La Traviata*'.

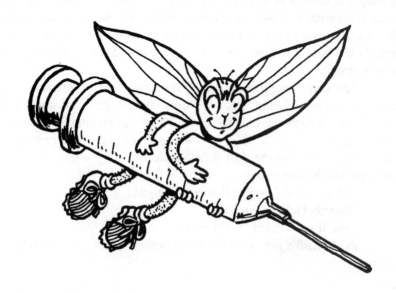

The female warrior

by Margaret Smith

Chironohld beings,
With such a nasty bite.
We try to leave them well alone,
But they attack on sight.

The male lives in the hedgerows,
For him we need no balm.
A gentle little creature,
Doing no-one any harm.

The female is the warrior
Who bites our arms and legs.
It's thought that she needs human blood
So she can lay her eggs.

We've tried all kinds of remedies,
But all to no avail;
Different creams and lotions,
— And every time we fail.

What is this tiny creature,
That lurks 'neath every bridge,
On riverbanks and hillsides?
It is, of course — the Midge.

They're busy — biting me!

by Margaret Smith

Why go abroad for holidays
To get your bites and stings?
For Scotland has the midges
And lots of other things.

From Gretna Green to John O' Groats,
From Stirling through to Skye
(Now re-named "The Midgy Isle"),
As for my blood they vie.

If they'd a competition
To find the biggest pest,
It would be a walkover,
The Scottish midge is best.

In warm and sultry weather,
No matter what I wear,
They get up skirts and trousers
And even in my hair.

I'm trying to export them
To France or Greece or Spain,
But they've a homing instinct
And all come back again.

To send the midges elsewhere
Would fill my wildest dreams,
I've tried all kinds of lotions,
Tinctures, jells and creams.

Repellent manufacturers
Go laughing to the bank.
They get rich at my expense,
The midge I have to thank.

So come to Bonnie Scotland
By air, by land, by sea,
Don't think about the midges,
They're busy — biting me.

A letter from a midgie wife

Hello dear reader, Minnie McMidge here! I'm glad to have this space to put the side of life from the point of view of we midges.

You know, we really are called the most dreadful names. Nasty little blighters. Won't give you a moment's peace. The scourge of mankind. I've been mortified lying on the ceiling of many a Highland hotel and listening to some of the things that are said about us.

As usual, of course, we women come off worst. Okay, I know our menfolk don't bite. In the land of the midge it is left to females such as myself to be the blood winners.

I think the good Lord knew what he was doing at Nature's creation when he devised this arrangement. He felt he could rely on us women to spot the cunning of humans, who will go to any lengths to avoid us.

It's quite shocking really, but folks in the Highlands and their visitors try and blow us out with pipe smoke... spray us with all sorts of lotions and potions... go about covered from head to toe in camouflage outfits. Even the Highland cattle are light brown coloured because it's a known fact that midgies home in on dark colours.

Now scientists are being paid a fortune in research grants to try and find a cure which will blow us off the face of the earth from Perth to Plockton.

They are all making sterling efforts but I'm not worried. I know that four hundred years ago American Indians used a certain plant as a way of getting rid of us, but in more recent times this particular plant has been found to be dangerous poison as far as humankind is concerned. And that brings me to my final point...

If you are digesting my words, dear reader, in some part of the Scottish Highlands or indeed in any territory which is fertile for us then beware.

THAT LITTLE BLACK SPECK ON THE CORNER OF THE PAGE COULD BE ME.

READY TO POUNCE!

A Fine Summer's Evening

by Roddy Maclean

"Tombaca!" — tobacco — **cried the old man as he watched the showers clearing over the islands. "I forgot to get tobacco."**

He removed a pot of bubbling soup from the peat-stove and went outside. The air was filled with the familiar heavy sweet smell of fresh rain mingling with the ever-present odour from his pet sheep.

"Ulysses", said the man, "teich as mo rathad" — get out of my way. The young Cheviot's entry to the house was barred — for the moment. The old man continued his lecture, informing Ulysses that his presence in the kitchen was required only after he had dried off. Calum MacDonald was getting soft, though, and soon the smell of wet, greasy, soiled wool would permeate his simple croft-house. Not that he really minded. After all, since the death of his beloved sheep-dog, Ulysses was his only friend, or so it often seemed in such a remote spot.

"Ach well, the summer is almost here", said Calum, but the sheep remained unconcerned and scampered past him to take up pride of position in the relative warmth of the kitchen. "I'll be taking a wee walk to the top of the Cnoc Ban."

His old legs carried him, crunching through the damp heather and a patch of verdant pasture, to a small hillock overlooking the house. The nearest settlement was seven miles to the south by path, a little township with a hotel, a post office and a scatter of whitewashed cottages facing the sea. It lay out of sight, round the green hills.

Calum loved the isolation, but today he was not a happy man. Even a casual observer would hardly have failed to notice from the old man's countenance that he was deeply disturbed. His expression took on a mood of apopletic abandonment when he looked at the acres of bracken-covered hillside behind the house.

"Cursed bracken", he muttered. "Cursed bracken!"

Calum turned to look south once more, gazing in appreciation at the pale evening light reflected in the numerous pools of freshly-collected water that lay on the meadow. Then a movement caught his eye — a flash of red about a mile away, moving along the track towards his house. Then another — this one blue. Two people.

"Ah-ha — maybe pipe smokers!" exclaimed the old man with a

touch of incautious optimism. His 68-year-old legs, suddenly sprightly and enthusiastic, carried him quickly back down to the croft.

He slipped off his Wellingtons and hurried across to the stove, moving the soup pot back on to the heat. Then he lifted his tweed cap, brushed his thinning hair neatly and slipped the cap on again, before going outside to prepare a welcome that would be warm, but not suspiciously insistent.

Calum could see the two walkers — a young man and woman both laden with camping gear — heading off the track towards his croft, so he picked up a spade, in order to look occupied, and wandered into the vegetable garden at the front of the house.

Soon the couple appeared at the garden wall.

"Ciamar a tha sibh?" ventured the newcomer, a tall slim man in his early twenties.

"Oh, tha gu math," replied Calum, lifting his eyebrows in surprise at hearing his native tongue. "Am bheil Gaidhlig agaibh?"

"Tha beagan. Tha mi ag ionnsachadh," the young man replied. There followed a lively discussion in Gaelic between the old man. who had spoken no other tongue until he was 15, and the young hillwalker, a Dundonian, who was teaching himself the language. His girlfriend, a small and slim woman whose head barely cleared the rough stone wall of the garden, obviously had little comprehension of the exchange and the two switched to English.

"I'm sorry", she said. "One day I'll learn to speak Gaelic. David here is going to teach me."

Calum invited the pair into the house. He was delighted to have company, especially as the visitors clearly had a great interest in him and his way of life. For two hours, over soup, scones and strong tea, they talked about crofting, fishing, gamekeeping and poaching. On one occasion, the old man distracted himself into relating stories of his distant exploits as a young seaman in the Merchant Navy, but the young couple brought him back to life in the Highlands. Calum was a living history book and they could not get enough of him.

Suddenly, the old man leapt to his feet. "A Dhia!" he exclaimed. "I had forgotten! Does either of you smoke a pipe?"

"Certainly not", replied the girl and immediately put a hand to her mouth, realising that she might have offended her host.

But he was not at all put out. "Life here can be murder without tobacco, especially at this time of year. I am so far from the village and I am getting old. Mail and provisions are brought in just once a month by boat and the next time is still three weeks away."

He looked expectantly at the young man, hoping for an offer of assistance. None was forthcoming.

"I tell you what", said Calum, the glint of imminent victory in his eye, "you can camp down by my beach for as long as you want if you go to the village tomorrow and bring me a month's supply of pipe tobacco."

The young couple conferred and, taken by the old crofter's plight and his offer, agreed to the suggestion.

The next day dawned fine and warm, and Calum wore a worried look as he shoved Ulysses out through the door from his place by the stove. He then swept up the droppings on the hearth and threw them on his garden.

"You won't be too long going to the village?" he queried when his guest came up to bid him good morning.

"What sort of tobacco would you like?" asked David.

"Let me see now", pondered the old man. "Yes, get Mahogany Flake, that's the blackest, tarriest, smokiest sort there is."

The young woman screwed up her nose at the thought of thick fumes mingling with the penetrating smell of sheep. The kitchen would be insufferable...

"I'll go to the village," said the young man. "Jean is to stay here. I'll be back before evening."

A short time later, he donned his boots and began to plod the track south towards the village. It was a delightful walk, sandwiched between the green hills and the silver sea sparkling in the sunshine.

Calum then took a fern hook and began to clear the bracken near the house, muttering and swearing as he went. It was hard work for an old man.

"You don't like the bracken?" ventured the young woman.

"Oh, it's dreadul stuff," came the reply.

"You'll see what I mean. It'll all start tonight, mark my words. Yes, tonight it will happen."

"What will happen?" asked Jean.

"It'll be alright, though, I'll have my tobacco", replied Calum, a smile creasing his ruddy, weather-beaten face. "But what will you do?"

"What do you mean, what will I do?" exclaimed the young woman, concern and consternation displaying themsleves in the tone of her voice.

"Och, there's no point in worrying you. I'm sure you'll be alright," replied the old man, mysteriously.

The topic was dropped and Jean went off to walk along the shore. When she returned, Calum was asleep in the old armchair by the peat fire. the pet sheep, for all the world like an adoring dog, reclining at his feet.

In the afternoon, David returned with an enormous supply of tobacco. As he walked into the house, the old crofter awoke and an enormous smile spread across his face.

"Ah, tombaca!" he exclaimed. "Moran taing, a bhalaich!" — many thanks to you.

Calum got out of the chair and began to rummage around in a cupboard, finally extracting an old pipe which he laid next to the tobacco on the table.

"You'll be dying for a smoke, I suppose," grinned the young man.

"No," was the simple response.

"But I thought you were in dire need of tobacco," David retorted.

"And I am," replied the old man, seriously.

"But surely you need a smoke," insisted the hillwalker, wondering about the necessity of his day's hike.

"No — well, only when the occasion demands," replied the crofter enigmatically. Sensing the tension that was building up, he added, "but I am most grateful for the tobacco, as you'll see this evening."

David and Jean sat mystified. What would happen in the evening?

As the shadows lengthened, the weather became still and breathless. It was very warm and the sea was like glass, bearing near-perfect reflections of the offshore islands. It was a flawless Highland summer evening. Flawless, that is, except for one thing...

"Here they come!" shouted Calum from the garden as he pulled the pipe out of his pocket, filled it with tobacco and lit it. David and Jean came running from their tent and were suddenly confronted by a hideous sight. A cloud of midges, containing thousands upon thousands of the tiny flying insects, emerged from the bracken to invade the garden and croft.

The young couple tried in vain to fight off the new arrivals while Calum sat on a chair in his garden, puffing vigorously on his pipe and producing enormous clouds of vile grey smoke which no midge dared enter.

"A fine summer's evening," he mused. "A fine summer's evening!"

Buzz words on the midge rampant

by Albert Morris

Let me commend to you M. **Auguste Henri Forel** (1848-1931), Swiss psychologist, professor of psychiatry at Zurich, an expert on the psychology of ants and a shrewd insect-watcher, who wrote, "It is possible, in insects, to demonstrate the existence of memory, of the association of sensory images, of perception, attention, habit-forming, the use of experience and other distinct though feeble evidences of deliberation and adaption."

As far as insects were concerned, there were no flies on M. Forel. He knew his subject and as one who all his life has been persecuted by such winged or non-flying creatures, bitten, stung or otherwise made uncomfortable by their attentions, I agree with the professor that they have a memory.

I would go further; I suspect that it is passed on genetically so that the descendants of some horse-fly that hounded me 20 years ago, know instinctively that they should come at me in swarms, with malicious intent, the moment I appear perspiring over some rustic horizon intent on getting back to nature and restoring my city-frayed tissues.

I enjoyed a walk in the Pentlands recently, not because I tramped over the wine-red moors blown by winds austere and pure, but because at this time of year there was not an insect about to get a quick bite and drink out of my system.

I am one of these unfortunates, beloved by insects of all species which pass up perfectly good opportunities to annoy other people so that they can peel-off out of the sun and dive-bomb me.

The Pentland Hills have flies deeply affectionate towards me and some summer days have seen me walking with my wife, I covered not in single spies but in battalions, followed by a joyous, buzzing wake of them, with my wife hardly bothered by one.

I to the hills will lift mine eyes to the flies. Many years ago, my head and arms liberally covered in an age-old insect repellent called *citronella* and carrying a high-tech aerosol insect spray in my rucksack, I rested on a heather-topped hill at Glen Sax, near Peebles.

With an angry buzz, about eight million flies rose in a huge cloud and came at me. The scent of *citronella* stung them to a fury and no matter how often I fired desperate bursts of repellent at them, they dived at me like

Second World War Japanese suicide pilots attacking a US aircraft carrier.

I have to admit that I was driven off the hill and pursued along the glen until I got into my car. Even then, a persistent fly that darted inside attacked me all the way home until I dispatched it with a lethal, rolled-up newspaper.

Belgian dramatist Maurice Maeterlinck wrote, "Something in the insect seems to be alien to the habits, morals and psychology of this world, as if it had come from some other planet, more monstrous, more energetic, more insensate, more atrocious, more infernal than our own."

Exactly so, and anyone who has spent some time in tropical climes will know the entomological horror of some of the creatures, red-eyed, many-winged-and-legged, fluttering, biting and crawling, that would drop from ceilings, crawl under doors or beat a barbaric tattoo with their wings on the windows.

Ah, the exquisite irritation felt after one had made elaborate preparations to place a mosquito net over one's bed, and then found that one of the family *Culcidae* was sharing your sleeping quarters, its whine, like a distant dentist's drill, keeping you making ineffectual passes through the night.

In Africa's sunny clime where I used to spend my time repelling assaults from hostile flies, unfriendly beetles and trying to establish a *cordon sanitaire* against spiders as big as saucers, British soldiers went through fearful ordeals with insects dropping chaotically on to their disciplined heads and laps and down their open shirts, but they came through heroically flailing in all directions and knowing that a little of swat they fancied did them good.

I can remember standing on parade and watching a small but energetic spider dangling from the front of my bush hat, intent on constructing a web like a gun-sight before my eyes.

These were not good days and some fine lads were reduced to gibbering wrecks when locusts found their way down their bush shirts, and others were never the same after sitting inadvertently on a route-marching colony of soldier ants.

Of all the insects that have raised bumps and itchy spots on me and drawn blood from my cringing skin, I suppose the Highland midge has caused me the greatest melancholy.

I can remember standing on a windless Celtic summer evening watching the hidden sun ring black Mull in a lake of fire. It was a time of prose inspiration and poetic derivation, lofty thoughts about man's place in the universe, and a hush like a benison, all ruined by the fact that local midges were working overtime and making me feel that hundreds of tiny hypodermic syringes were being plunged into my face.

Like most people, I have tried a witch's brew of creams and other repellents to make midges, if not curl up and die, at least pause in their tracks. All to no avail.

Ancients, wise in the ways of midges, told me that smoke from a pipe tobacco called Navy Cut plug was effective in thwarting them temporarily — rather like a destroyer making smoke for protective purposes — but that fag smokers just suffered.

That was not strictly true. Once I smoked black Burmese cheroots and had crafty drags at Balkan cigarettes, both of which gave out smoke redolent of Eastern bazaars, seraglio nights and a faint whiff of lodging house cat.

The midges seemed stunned by the effects of passive smoking and one sensed that they were suddenly coughing and wiping their eyes. After a pause of about 20 minutes, though, they seemed to be getting used to the scent, perhaps even inhaling it with enjoyment, and then having a quiet drink off you as a chaser.

According to a report, zoologists at Aberdeen University have been given a grant of over £53,000 by the Agriculture and Food Research Council to study the airborne chemical messages, called pheromones, that midges use to attract the opposite sex.

If the love calls can be identified, synthetic pheromones could be used to lure the ardent swains and pulsating females into traps where they could be disposed of, presumably with the equivalent of a humane killer.

While I hope Aberdeen zoologists are successful, it does occur to me that one of the reasons why many scenic areas of the Highlands have not been turned into industrial estates, new towns, developments by speculative builders, time-share outcrops and theme parks is the persistent and possibly patriotic midge. Perhaps we should be thankful for it.

Meanwhile, a school of fearful thought is growing that one day insects will take over the world. If so, I hope they will remember with gratitude how I always took them along on all my picnics.

A watery grave

by Jane Struth

After only five minutes of gardening
two showers later and
a skin covered
in itchy red blotches
I am pacing in front of the
window watching a warm
summer's evening being destroyed
by swarms of 'king midges'.

Every so often a stray one
batters into the window and I
roar with Wembley ferocity
as its meagre body falls apart
and slides picturesquely
down the window pane.

One by one the kids troop in
itchy red and angry
flabbergasted at being defeated
by such small opponents
"It's only a wee fly too"
they innocently wail.

Lastly being unable to reach the door
husband blunders in through the
window his light blue sweater
turned black by a coat of midges
attracted by colour — or sweat
he stands under the shower
fully clothed cursing the wee monsters
to their watery grave.

Midgies hit the headlines!

The Queen's husband had a close encounter with a midgie at Holyrood Palace. One landed on his lips while he was presenting gold awards to young winners of his awards scheme.

Reported the *Daily Record*: He swept it away and it ended up on his hand. He was about to swat it when he said: "As president of the Wildlife Fund I can hardly kill it." He then carefully put it on the lawn.

And the *Sunday Mail* told how a minister's wife came to the rescue when the Queen Mother was attacked during Highland Games at the Castle of Mey in Caithness.

According to the paper those near to the Queen Mother noticed she was being bitten when she began rubbing her legs and waving the tiny insects away from her face. A woman sitting nearby whipped out a midge spray from her handbag and applied it to the Royal legs. A rug was brought in but the little blighters were not to be outdone. The attack continued until the entire Royal party were forced to seek open ground.

Aberdeen scientists won a £53,000 grant to research air-borne chemical messages sent out by midgies. Called pheromones, they may be used to communicate, alarm, attract mates, establish swarms or transmit many other details, reported the *Scottish Daily Express*.

But, said the *Express*, the cash may not be sufficient to clip the wings of the insects whose razor-sharp bite has driven millions to distraction.

"No miracle cures are possible for the Scottish midge," declared the doctor leading the investigation team.

An anti-midge jacket, consisting of a cotton string vest with a hood, can be imported from the United States for around £20, according to the *Sunday Mail*. It may look like a joke — but it's impregnated with a repellent which actually works.

Islanders on Barra were furious over a bank's TV commercial which claimed that midgies on the *Whisky Galore!* isle were bigger than anywhere else. It declared that local midgies were as big as a sparra (sparrow). The bank later apologised for any offence which may have been caused.

A university lecturer called for a warning in all tourist brochures about the midgie menace. "People should be alerted so they equip themselves with the right ointments... they come here with no knowledge of the beasts and are taken unaware," he said.

Two students allowed themselves to be eaten alive by midgies and clegs as part of their university degree course. The *Record* told how they'd taken a cottage on Loch Aweside, Argyll, to study the habits of the double curse of Scotland. One allowed armies of midgies to settle on his forearm while the other let clegs bite away.

MIDGIES STOP PLAY was a classic headline in the *Daily Telegraph*. Players ran from the field as swarms of midgies made a biting attack during their game. "They swarmed in to bite like tigers and there was no way cricket could be played," said one of the organisers. "Some of the players had lumps as big as cricket balls."

When the game was reconvened players took to the field armed with insect repellents.

Grant aid to put the bite on midges

Researchers are working on an anti-midge repellent that makes people invisible to their tormentors, reported the *Scottish Daily Express* in March, 2003. The team from the University of Aberdeen were awarded a £150,000 grant by Scottish Enterprise to design a repellent that will fool the midgies into thinking that various chemicals on our skin are not present.

Dr Jennifer Mordue, head of the team which has spent 12 years searching for ways to beat the midgie, told the *Scottish Daily Mirror*: "We have a great understanding of the biology of midges and how they find their victims. We are hoping to identify the chemicals in the sweat which makes some people more susceptible to being bitten."

It is also hoped that the repellent can be modified for use on disease-spreading midges in the Third World.

Saved by our breeks!

Eric Allison receives a bulging postbag every year from folk recounting close encounters of the midgie kind and suggesting possible ways to see off the little blighters. These letters are a selection from his mailbag...

At the weekly pipe band practice our Pipe Major decided it was too fine an evening to practise in the drill hall — he suggested instead we should march a mile to Woodcot, the old folks' home, and entertain the residents.

His idea met with instant approval. Glad to be out of the stuffy hall, we formed up outside, 12 pipers and six drummers, struck up *Highland Laddie* and off we set to our rendezvous with the old folk.

Locals turned out to cheer us along the way and at the home we marched and countermarched while the residents appeared on the flower-bedded front lawn. *The Barren Rocks of Aden* and *Highland Wedding* were among the tunes we played, followed by strathspeys and reels.

Then the Pipe Major led us further along the road to a point where it was completely overhung with trees. I thought to myself, 'Boy, you are asking for trouble' — for I could see the road ahead of us was shrouded by clouds of midges continuously swooping from the river into the wood and back again.

The Pipe Major must have had elephant hide for the midges did not seem to have any effect on him. He marched and coutermarched us through the cloud of midges quite unaware of the devastating effect they were having on us! They were in our hair, eyes, ears, neck, hands and everywhere else they could find blood. I could only thank God that we were in long trews...

I SHUDDERED TO THINK WHERE THEY WOULD HAVE GONE IF WE HAD BEEN WEARING OUR KILTS.
Stirling piper.

Midgies have been the bane of my life whenever I visited the Highlands but since last year I have managed to repel them by the simple measure of rubbing *Cedar Wood* aftershave into my skin. A fisherman friend has another remedy. His wife provides him with a piece of chiffon which he swathes round his head, tucking it well into his neck. He maintains this allows him to see through the material and enjoy his fishing without any bother from midgies.
Glasgow pensioner

Use your own saliva to combat the midgies. Wet your fingers and rub your brow or wherever. If your saliva runs dry rub the back of your ears to induce it to run freely. If all this fails pretend you have a sneezy cold and get a steamy bowl of menthol going... then sit on your garden chair and enjoy yourself.

P.S. It doesn't always work!

Housewife. Biggar, Lanarkshire.

I would like to recount an amusing story involving the demon midgie, which happened to me some time ago when I was a teenager. It was a long hot summer, and I was camping with a number of others in an outward bound camp near Oban. The organisers decided it would help develop our characters if we assisted the Forestry Commission clear thick woodland so that a new access road could be built.

We duly arrived at the site dressed in shorts and casual shirts. It was a glorious day. Our mode of dress was a source of great amusement to the handful of forestry workers who were all kitted out in heavy overalls and long sleeved shirts. We were about to find out why they were so amused!

As we started to chop down the undergrowth we were severely set upon by clouds of ferocious midgies. They attacked every inch of our bare flesh. My friends and I beat a hasty retreat to the main road, and into a nearby loch, but we were too late as the damage had been done. My face was so badly bitten and swollen that my eyes were almost closed.

Later that day a group of us took an excursion into Oban. A local fisherman asked why my face was so badly swollen and I told him all about the attack. He went on to the deck of his boat and poured liquid from a red coloured can onto an oily rag and told me to smear it over my face. I did and in an instant my face was on fire. My eyes throbbed. I thought I had blinded myself and started to scream. A crowd gathered and amid the commotion the fisherman told me that the rag was soaked in diesel oil, and that I was supposed to take it out the bag when the midgies were biting, put a match to it, and swing it above my head to keep them away!

I was really embarrassed as everyone except me thought the situation was hysterical, so I sneaked off and disappeared into the tourist traffic. I have not related this story until now!

Uddingston traveller.

Midgie bite

by Adam Harvey

We'd spent a marvellous day, alright,
Noo tired, or drunk, at nine at night.
There must've been eighty or ninety of us
At Largs pier waiting for the bus.
Some had sailed to Millport
Across the silvery sea
Then took the ferry back again
To Nardini's for their tea.
Some had drunk a wheen o' jars
Pub crawling roon the local bars
Noo staunin' wearying for hame
Twas then, by God, the midgies came.
Came swarming doon, a great black cloud,
And landed on the patient crowd
To stir up waves of raw emotion
And cause a terrible commotion.
Wiping heads and scratching faces
Fingers fumbling in intimate places
Baritone shouts and soprano cries
Boobs and bums and fleshy thighs
This flapping, wriggling, squirming mass
Suffered a midgie *coup de grace*
While passers by with casual glance
Mistook it for some African dance.
At last, two buses came along
To rescue the demented throng
Who cried with voices shrill with fright
There's nothing worse than a midgie bite!

The biter bitten

by Jeff Torrington

"Adam and Eve," hissed the Snake,
"This Apple is truly delicious."
"Nay," says the First Born, "we maunna partake,
Tis against the Heid Gairdener's wishes."
But the Serpent Eve's lughole was nippin',
"Pray, eat, 'tis omniscient fruit.
All Knowing's contained in this Pippin."
So Eve bit — that was it — now we'd rue it!
For Knowledge proved bitter and tough,
At their crime all of Eden was tuttin',
Cried Adam: "We're baith in the buff!
And wumman — whaur's thy belly-button?"
But Eve who for long had been simmering
At being made from a chauvinist's rib,
Now began to see the first glimmering
Of what would become Women's Lib.
"Tae think I wance called you the 'Big Chief,'"
She sighed with the guile of a vixen,
And handed her mate a wee fig-leaf
Which he tore in half before fixin'.
Now along came Eden's Big Parkie,
Saw how the genders each strove,
Quoth he in a rage: "What's the lark, eh?
This is Eden — no ruddy Beechgrove!"
The quarrelsome pair he ejected,
Far from Eden's lush ridges,
Saying: "Gang ye baith forth unprotected
'Gainst aw biting things — specially midges!"
So the franchise was given al fresco
Whether on flat lands or hilly
For gnats to use man as a Tesco,
A food source that slaps itself silly.
Self-flagellation with deep remorse smitten,
'Tis a fate not without its grim beauty,
For thus is the fruit-biter bitten
By the Midge on celestial duty!

All over the world, her cousins are biting tonight!

A fascinating insight into the world of the midgie and its vast family of relatives is given by three British Museum experts in *British Blood-sucking Flies* (published in 1939).

Family: CERATOPOGONIDAE
(BITING MIDGES; in North America known as PUNKIES or sometimes as SANDFLIES.)
The small flies which comprise this family were, until somewhat recently, included with other non-biting flies in the larger family Chironomidae, the two groups having many features in common; the separation, however, is now generally agreed upon and is both convenient and natural, the biting midges having in fact rather more in common with the Simuliidae than with the Chironomidae. As in the case of the Simuliidae, the females of all Ceratopogonidae possess well-developed biting mouth-parts, including a pair of toothed mandibles which work on the "scissors" principle; such structures are absent in the Chironomidae. The flies are all small or minute in size, usually of slender build, with wings superimposed over the back when at rest. The males (which do not bite) resemble those of Culcidae and Chironomidae and differ from those of Simuliidae in having bushy antennae. The wing-venation is of a simplified type and on a rather uniform plan throughout the family.

In Britain nearly 150 species of Ceratopogonidae are known to exist. Fortunately the great majority of these do not use their mandibles for the purpose of obtaining animal blood. Nearly half of them are known or believed to subsist by capturing and devouring other small insects; many more feed, so far as is known, mainly or solely upon flower juices. Of those which do suck blood some members of the genus Fordpomya attack only smooth, juicy caterpillars, others pierce the wing-veins of butterflies, moths, lace-wing flies or dragonflies; others, in America, attack stick insects; one European species of the genus Atrichopogon confines its diet to the blood of oil-beetles, and another species of the same genus in South India has been found sucking mealy-bugs. Probably future research will reveal a still

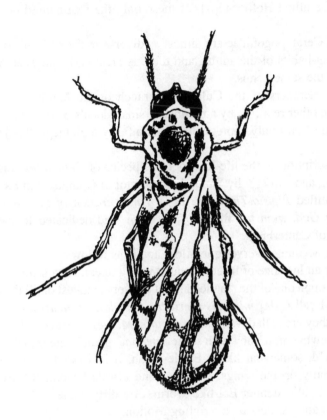

AN ACCURATE DRAWING OF
THE MIDGIE FEEDING,
HER WINGS CROSSED SCISSOR-LIKE
OVER HER ABDOMEN.

Drawing by David Braysher, after Ross Richards.

greater variety of feeding-habits in the family. The habit of sucking the blood of mammals or birds has only been definitely established as occurring in three genera of this family, Culicoides, Lasiohelea, and Leptoconops (including the allied Holoconops); of these only the first-named occurs in Britain.

The Ceratopogonidae are almost as diverse in their life-histories as in the feeding-habits of the adults, and there is great variation even among members of the same genus.

The members of the Culicoides branch of the family are distinguished from other relatives by a number of small details of structure which are for the most part only appreciable under a fairly high magnification.

The first description of the life-history of a species of *Culicoides* was published as long ago as 1713, by W. Derham, Rector of Upminster in Essex, in his work entitled *Physio-Theology: or a demonstration of the being and attributes of God, from his Works of Creation*, and dedicated to the then Archbishop of Canterbury.

This account deserves quotation, and is as follows:

"For an Instance of Insects endued with a Spear, I shall, for its peculiarity, pitch upon one of the smallest, if not the very smallest of all the *Gnat*-kind, which I call *Culex minimus nigricans maculatus sanguisuga*. Among us in Essex they are called *Nidiots*, by *Mouffet Midges*. It is about 1/10 of an inch, or somewhat more long with short *antennae*, plain in the female, in the male feather'd, somewhat like a Bottle-brush. It is spotted with blackish spots, especially on the wings, which extend a little beyond the Body. It comes from a little slender Eel-like Worm, of a dirty white Colour, swimming in stagnating waters by a wrigling Motion.

"Its *Aurelia* (pupa) is small, with a black Head, little short Horns, a spotted, slender rough Belly. It lies quietly on the top of the Water, now and then gently wagging itself this way and that.

"These Gnats are greedy Blood-suckers, and very troublesome where numerous, as they are in some places near the *Thames*, particularly in the Breach-waters that have lately befallen near us, in the Parish of Dagenham; where I found them so vexatious, that I was glad to get out of those marshes. Yea, I have seen Horses so stung with them, that they have had drops of Blood all over their Bodies, where they were wounded by them."

The eggs of *Culicoides* are cigar-shaped or sometimes banana-shaped, dark in colour, and laid singly or in small groups; in some species at least they are capable of withstanding prolonged periods of dryness. The larvae, which in the larger species attain a maximum length of about 9 mm, are provided with an oval pale brownish head and a long, smooth, dull whitish or translucent body which terminates in a few hairs; they progress with a snake-like motion. Though the larvae of most species of *Culicoides* are normally aquatic, these can survive for at least six days in moist situations where no free water is present; moreover, some species appear to pass their whole existence in moist soil, and others in moist decaying vegetable matter without any appreciable content of water; those of a Japanese species breed in the dung of the poultry which it attacks. The aquatic species spend the greater part of their time buried in the fine mud at the bottom, with the front part of the body protruding. The duration of larval life varies with climatic conditions and with the species; in the case of the salt marsh species of North America, a study concluded that the larvae live for at least six months if not for a whole year, and that they flourished best at rather low temperatures.

The pupae are provided with small breathing-horns on the thorax, and rows of spines on the abdomen; they are capable of very little movement, merely turning the end of the abdomen about like the Chrysalis of a moth; usually they may be found floating passively on the surface of the water; they breathe air and are incapable of surviving long submersion in water. The duration of the pupal stage is from three to seven days.

Species of *Culicoides* are found in most parts of the world, except (apparently) in Patagonia and New Zealand, and the blood-sucking habit appears to be universal, birds as well as mammals being attacked. There appear to be no records at present of attacks by midges on reptiles or amphibia, but an interesting variation of the blood-sucking habit is found in an Oriental species which obtains its food from the body of a gorged mosquito instead of directly from a mammalian host.

In some countries the annoyance caused by midges is extremely serious, and deaths have even been attributed to their bites (in Belgium, reported by Goetghebuer, 1919), though it is probable that in such cases the real cause of death was blood-poisoning by subsequent infection of a scratch.

Considering the abundance and ferocity of many midges, it is perhaps surprising that there is as yet little evidence incriminating them in the spread of disease. Evidence has however accumulated in recent years show-

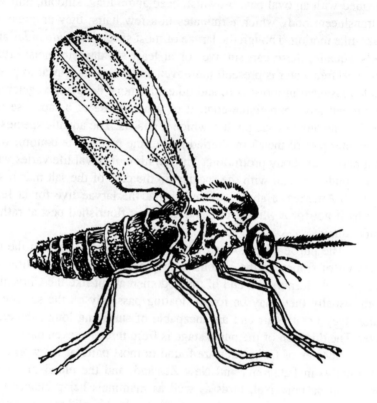

**THIS IS HOW SHE REALLY LOOKS
UNDER THE MICROSCOPE.
MIDGIE IN FLIGHT, READY FOR A FEED!.**

Drawing by David Braysher, after Ross Richards.

ing that species of *Culicoides* are intermediate hosts of certain filarial worms which pass part of their life in the blood of mammals.

The irritation and annoyance caused by the attacks of midges is often so great as to constitute a serious problem. Their numbers are in some countries sufficient to make outdoor work impossible, and they may seriously interfere with tourist business at seaside resorts. It has been suggested that their abundance on the coasts of Florida and other southern states of North America has been largely the cause of the lack of early development of these areas; and also that the backward condition of croft farming in western Scotland may be partly due to their very harmful activities. Certain it is that they constitute a major pest in parts of Scotland as well as in the West Indies.

As in the case of mosquitoes, the effect of the bites varies with different victims as well as with the species of midge; on some persons the disagreeable sensations caused by the bites are transitory, the only after-effect being a small red spot on the skin, but on others (especially women) weals are raised which may cause great discomfort for two or three days. B. Jobling (1928), who is evidently a susceptible subject, thus summarises the effects upon himself of the bites of three species of *Culicoides*:

"The intense initiation caused by the bite of *Culicoides* begins at the moment of piercing, and lasts from one to several days according to the species. Scratching the skin increases the irritation as well as the size of the swelling and prolongs their duration. Moreover, by scratching, it is very easy to tear the skin from the swelling; the resulting sore heals much more slowly than a sore produced by an accidental cut or scratch, being also liable to bacterial infection. The irritation and swelling caused by the bite of *C. puiicaris* is of very short duration and in many cases disappears on the following day, whereas the bite of *C. vexans*, and more particularly of *C. obsoletus*, produces a more intense irritation, which may last more than a week, the swelling being very distinct on the second and in many cases even the third day after the bite."

Jobling further remarks that "if the lesion is moistened and rubbed with a crystal of sodium carbonate, the irritation ceases in a few seconds, and does not recur. Furthermore, the swelling also subsides very rapidly. The same result is obtained even if the application is not made till twenty-four hours have elapsed."

Some form of protection from the attacks of *Culicoides* is often highly desirable if not essential. Screening is difficult owing to the minute size of the insects, but some form of mask provided with a respirator might sometimes be used with advantage by outdoor workers. Smudges and repellents are much used by holiday makers. In regard to the former, tobacco smoke is usually helpful, but it has been found that a more efficient alternative in keeping a tent clear of midges is the smoke from burning incense. A great variety of repellents has been suggested for application to the skin or hair, but most of them are transitory in their effects, and some are unsuitable for general use.

The following are among those recommended:

(a) A mixture of oil of lavender, 1 part, and elder-flower water, 20 parts (recommended by a writer in Home Gardening, May 1928; said to be very efficacious, one application lasting a whole evening).

(b) Oil of pennyroyal (recommended by J. G. Myers in West Indies).

(c) A mixture of oil of thyme, 1 part, concentrated extract of pyrethrum flowers in mineral oil, 2 parts, and castor or olive oil, 5 parts (recommended by C. Graham MacMay in Canadian Entomologist, August 1938).

(d) Oil of white birch is effective, but its odour is unpleasant.

(e) Citronella, 1 oz, liquid petroleum, 4oz (recommended by R. Matheson as least injurious to the skin).

(f) Oil of cassia, 1 oz, brown oil of camphor, 2 oz, lanoline, 3oz, paraffin wax to stiffen (recommended by Bacot and Talbot 1919; confirmed by A. W. McKenny Hughes).

Dear Sir — We don't sting! A Protest

by Kath Hardie

A STIRLING MIDGIE PROTESTS OVER ERIC ALLISON'S
ANNUAL MIDGIE COMPETITION

STIRLING FESTIVAL - COMPETITION!

TELL US YOUR WORST
EXPERIENCE WITH
THE PERNICIOUS
SCOTTISH MIDGY AND
OTHER MAN-EATING
INSECTS IN CARTOONS,
HUMOROUS TALES
OR VERSE.

I have been asked to protest, in the strongest terms, about the current insect competition being held in the Continent of Stirling. And even, I learn, in the surrounding archipelagoes of Bannockburn and Whins of Milton.

As one of the few midges who can write, I speak for all my clan and other insect clans when I say, more in sadness than in anger, that we find the tone and the implications of this competition deeply offensive.

At a Grand Meeting held in Outer Raploch, brother-insects echoed these sentiments. Baron Barney of the Kingspark Blackflies (a noble breed), Count Hugo of the Hunting St Ninian's Hornets and Chief Murdo of the Muckhart Midges wished it to be known how angry and distressed they are by the blatant misrepresentation of the insect activities and traditions as portrayed in this competition.

In other words, they do not like it. Not at all...

The cause of this distress? First of all, the cartoon which accompanies the advertisement, of which more details anon. A crude picture of an insect who is, would you believe, engaged in the dubious activity of reading a book.... a book with more than one page. *(Publisher's note: Oops! As reproduced on our cover!)* This transgresses the teaching of our Great Philosopher and Teacher Midge PROPING MIRE THE SILENT who laid down that no midges were to read books without a good reason. For some positive reason (in my case to defend our rights, for example). Otherwise it is an almighty time-wasting activity.

The title of this foul book suggests we sting friends. First of all, we never sting and secondly, if we did, we would never sting friends.

Then humans are invited to desribe their encounters with our clan — and this wounds deeply — in a humorous fashion. Our history tells us that there has never been anything even remotely amusing in such close encounters of the midge kind.

What is worse is the appellation of "man-eating" or "flesh-eating" which is usually bestowed on us by humans who rarely desist from placing themselves in front of plates of flesh of all kinds, hot and cold more than once in any day. How preposterous!

It is only too clear, that in the Continent of Stirling (and its surrounding archipelagoes of Bannockburn and Whins of Milton) at any rate, the works or our great scientist, Erik Midge von Einstein, are completely unknown.

He proves conclusively, and without a shadow of doubt (there is no disputing his words... in other words), that insects never sting and never eat flesh of any kind, much less human flesh.

This is accepted throughout the great Midge World everywhere. What is not accepted, nay not even generally known, is that humans for all their gigantic proportions, have ridiculously delicate skin. So frail and completely lacking in protection is this skin that it only requires one or two insects to alight, harmlessly, on it than it reacts in the most alarming way, changing colour, coming out in mounds and protuberances of flesh, and thereby irritating the human involved. This has disastrous consequences, need I point out, for all the poor harmless insects involved. Thousands of our midges, for example, have been slaughtered by the large shovel-like hairless paws taking an angry swipe at us.

What we find hard to tolerate is the way these humans wander uninvited into our territory and then protest that we are their enemy. As Erik Midge von Einstein repeats, the midge is a persecuted species and we do not like it. We do not like it at all!

And therefore, I trust you to take note of my protest and desist (even stop) from this competition, so damaging to the image of insects, not only in the Continent of Stirling (and its surrounding archipelagoes of Bannockburn and Whins of Milton) but to insects in the faraway Continents of Plean and Fallin, Tullibody and Tillicoultry... Do not provoke us... we are peaceful and gentle... but for how long?

In conclusion. I quote from our great rallying song —
Midges lived e'er Wallace led
Hornets off to London went
In Bannockburn some blackflies bled
During victory —

We love weed and we love flower
We can increase hour by hour
Men must stay far from our bower
To remain sting-free...

We eat neither man nor beast
We throw scorn on such a feast
Don't insult us — for at least —
We've always been free.

We love weed and we love flower
We can increase hour by hour
Men must stay far from our bower
To remain sting-free...

Barely time for a bite

by David Goldie

The clump from a discarded tackety boot was contemptuously familiar to me. Dull noises. It was synonymous with the coming home of Mother. Other families underwent a similar ritual of the slamming of a door to announce the exclusion of the working environment and the return of the breadwinner but our home always echoed to the disdainful prising off of leather and the scraping of the hobnails.

That day they not only announced Mother's expectation of food but also an impending confrontation between her and me, her daughter Glenda. My mind meandered temporarily, if furniture was symbolic of its owner then Mother would have had stools. Those long upright ones which say "American Diner" and fast food where people are served and guzzle quickly, without much pleasure and the emphasis is on process rather than product. That was deep thinking meritorious of those furtive hours watching Open University programmes. Like a petrol station where someone shouts "fill me up buddy," Mother stuffed herself in anticipation of the next session of work and it was a solitary cramming for Father and I stood merely in attendance. It was not a selfish act of exclusiveness but a representative monopoly of the society which was so undemocratically matriarchal and within this micrcosm Mother was queen.

It was one of those dog-days of high humidity and dullness which was idyllic under the trees that were home for us all. Anything but the most essential action would ensue and conversation from Mother, who was not subtle in character, would be squeezed from her line by line. Her nature was comparable to her physique which was brooding muscle and sinew that lacked any aesthetic aspects. She zigged, then zagged, and arrived at her tea. Within the world of the maneaters, she occasionally alluded to herself as Gene Kelly.

Routine dictated that talk had a tendency to begin sometime after the first mouthful of food. Victuals, then conversation. As usual, she would begin by flippantly informing us that it had been a good/bad day depending on the variables such as smoke or pesticides. "Mmmm," she said as her cheeks became expanding pouches, "shit hot is this!"

"Mother", I said, "syntax!" It was not meant as criticism. Jimmy Dean was no role model for me. As surely as it had come out automatically, repercussions would follow.

Yet Mother was a series of paradoxes. On one hand, she considered herself an artiste who was an integral part of the Scottish cultural spectrum but running concurrently against this was the nature of her work which brutalised her with its form of repetitiveness. It was piecework without finesse in a field where competition was intense, even this break would be long past before the shadows lengthened or changed by degree. The result of this inequation was stress which was channelled back upon us and I did not wish to perpetuate the cliche of being an entertainer on a conveyor belt.

"Does my offspring wish to put her tuppence worth in? Amuse me with your erudite views for today and don't tell me how or when to speak, mouth full or mouth empty. I am your mother and breadwinner. Therefore I am entitled to be the one who dictates the rules."

I lowered my heavy fledgling head and muttered that I was only making a point about the usage of language. Mother the piranha teased, "Language, san midge, sandwich, piece work. That dear daughter is called word association." Mimicry left me with nothing more to say.

By a quirk of birth, Father had been born a man and thus became genealogically subliminal to his wife and daughter because of their long snouts inherent in women of this society. I loved Father for his gentleness and his talent of guiding a conversation without the maternal confrontation. His methods were the implicit use of inference and insinuation and it seemed that Mother bullied him at every opportunity and yet at times she would treat him affectionately and call him "Little Hooter".

My train of thought was broken as Mother shouted rhetorically at Father, "What is this junk?"

"What does it look like?" said Father gamely as he merged invisibly with the gloom, muttering something perhaps inflammatory but definitely inaudible.

Hattie, for that was my Mother's first name continued. "And where did you get this? I know where it came from. You borrowed it from those fly middens from next door that we have for neighbours."

Father declared that there had not been time to shop around. Mother again interjected, "Farquhar, do I look like a vegetarian?" and an organic piece of matter slithered from her jaws. "I am a bloody hard worker and a carnivore. Is it so much to ask to get something substantial on the table?"

Just like Morel from Bestwood, I thought. This did not seem the most appropriate time to make my announcement but there is never an appropriate time to declare change and cause ructions and flaunt the traditions of a caste society. I had previously played out the scene in my mind thinking of suitable alternative answers to stem the impending maternal storm. I paused and watched her. She was slavering over the meal before zooming off to complete her shift. Past the period of incubation and no longer a tadpole, there was no appropriate moment. And I was at least one moon old.

"Mother, I don't want to be like you. I want to learn. I want to be a student."

The sound of the saliva breaking her food, reminiscent of a blocked drain, went silent and a tension consumed the distance between us as Mother hypnotically stared and I pretended not to wilt. Hattie's aphony and the accompaniment of the sound of Father's shuffling feet were the first immediate responses to my affirmation that I wanted and needed to conquer new horizons and make something of my life. I was out of mothballs or at least out of the closet because I had said it. I didn't want to be a face worker dependent upon my feminine muscles. I wanted to use my brain.

The declaration became anticlimactical being consumed into nothingness as the expected explosion of vitriol never materialised. I began to think that I had misconstrued Mother for she appeared almost mothlike, caught for an instant in the light and dazzled.

Then her head began to oscillate ponderously, becoming more animated and violent as she seemed to catalogue and assimilate the effects of such a draconian step upon the social apex.

I had anticipated a stream of accusations to be punctuated with the Caesarian cut "Et tu Glenda?" but instead I was given a long oral history of our clan, the family *Culicidae* who had divided into the *Culex molestus* and ourselves, the *Aedes punctor* and that there was a tradition to be upheld. These conventions were not made sterile by her but were vibrant necessities and for me to opt on the path of a thinker was not merely to go against the family but against nature itself.

"The skin of the man of letters is peculiarly sensitive to the bite of the critical mosquito; and he lives in a climate in which such mosquitoes swarm. He is seldom stabbed to the heart — he is often killed by pinpricks."

By staring in bewilderment at Farquhar who had interrupted, Mother and I had included him in a triangular discussion that would have been termed women's talk at the exclusion of his weaker sex.

"Alexander Smith", continued Father in answer to a question that had never been asked. Mother turned her behind to him. He may have had the weak and feeble body of a man and was thus a smaller animal than the rest of us but she should not treat him always so derogatively as the door-mat. An empathy that had already existed was strengthened at that moment between Dad and I through sharing the same resistance and because of it I became bold.

"Please do not treat Father as if he was some Kafkaesque carica-ture."

"Glenda, do not refer to your Father as a dung-beetle." Even Farquhar referred to himsef in the third person from habit, as if he was some distant body and not part of the company.

"I am not deserting anything. I want to increase, not destroy, our culture." These slogans seeemed to roll from my mouth and become redun-dant in the face of Mother who looked at me with warning as her attention ricocheted back from Father to me. It was an ominous glance which chal-lenged me to heed tradition, particularly Hymn 18, and know my place instead of those smutty books about coarse mosquitoes. To have explained it was actually Mosquito Coast seemed pointless.

"I am proud of what I am Mother and where I come from. But why do you always treat me like I'm still a larvae. Look at me, I'm a mature, con-senting midgy and I've moved a long way from that and still want to keep moving."

Mother ruminated both the last of her meal and what I had said and then became eloquent. "If God had intended that you read for a living then you would have been hatched with spectacles grafted onto you at birth but instead He gave you a long proboscis which can entertain by puncturing and bleeding. In our little country we may not be like some of our foreign rela-tives, for our days of causing malaria and ague are gone. And we are not exalted like our kith in Honduras where the Indians have adopted the name Miskito or the Rumanians who thought we originated from the smoke of the devil's pipe but we do hold a place in the cultural pecking order of tartan accomplishments.

"You think because I am a musclewoman that in itself is a stigma. I don't think so. I think I sell my power in a similar manner to the gymnast or professional athlete and have just as short a performing life and within the restrictions of perpetual backshift, I have freedom so that it is not merely a case of conditioning. I am like some emergency service who is expected to be there and without my presence there would be an incomplete whole...

> *The convenience of the high trees*
> *The air's buoyancy and the sun's ray*
> *Are of advantage to me;*
> *And the earth's face upward for my inspection."*

That was Ted Hughes that Mother had just quoted and then she went on to admit that she was not articulate and that what it boiled down to was a compact between insects and humans and that our value was estimated by the amount of minor irritation we were able to cause to those persons larger than ourselves. I was confused, a confused adolescent midgy.

It was Father's voice which again broke the brooding silence as he cleared the food away.

"I understand what you want to do but you must also appreciate your Mother's standpoint and not bite the hand that feeds you. I think it was an American, but it doesn't matter, who said something to the effect that whatever we do in summer, there are always the flies and if we walk in the woods, we must feed the mosquitoes. To change anything, you must work from within the system and we are part of a relatively unchanging order which dictates how Mother will react instinctively."

To Father, Mother was an artiste who loved the greasepaint and the smell and roar of the crowd for each performance, whether it be matinee or evening show. She was as Scottish as shortbread or Irn Bru. What would a picnic be without the perpetual irritation from a troupe of pirouetting mothers and it is from these air displays and the amount of debate and controversy that they produce, that they can be judged.

On that premise, for Farquhar, Hattie was anything but a failure. She was a successful performer who in conversation was only pipped by the weather. I was in a quandary because I did not disapprove of Mother's lifestyle but it was difficult for her to comprehend. I wanted to pronounce my feelings for them both because I think I understood what Father had meant. Academic work, even if successful, would have only limited success within a limited scope. To maximise the name of midgy was to follow in Mother's angles. However with almost theatrical precision the distant sound of air brakes floated up and both parents' senses honed upon it. The lull was over. Father looked to her like the stage dresser that he was and she wiped away the crumbs. They were two opposing halves that made a whole and that was me. He looked at her once more and said "Showtime" and she was gone.

I peered down as Mother's definition became no more than a dot among so many other dots which had congregated. It was tourists. The level of conversation grew louder as they settled at the picnic tables which were scattered with well ordered abandon around the base of our tree. High tea al fresco. It was the summer odours of fish suppers and vinegar, of cream cakes and laughter. I began to strain like a child hearing an ice cream van.

"Your Mother's a piranha among midgies," said Father. "But another snout would come in handy." He seemed to smile wistfully as I balanced on the edge of the lip of the nest but it was no snap decision I had arrived at as I pushed off shouting, "Wait for me, Mother, I'm coming too!"

Yes, the midgie can be beaten!

**If you go down to the woods during June, July, August or early
September it is more than likely that calls of "Timber!" will be drowned
out by the pained cries of "Oh no, not those damn midges again!"**

For it is during these weeks that the little blighters strike with relent-
less and absolute ferocity. Forests are their favourite restaurants. For a start
these places are their main larval breeding grounds.

The midges don't like bright sunlight so the shadowy atmosphere
created by the trees gives them a perfect environment in which to enjoy their
blood meals. It also explains why their key times of attack are dawn and
towards dusk — an early breakfast on humans will see them through until
the mid evening when dinner can consist of a German tourist for a starter,
followed by some Englishmen for the main course and a kilted Highlander
for dessert.

Seriously though, experts reckon that of all industries possibly
forestry comes off the worst from midge assaults. Half a century ago the use
of citronella as a repellent was widespread.

This is a yellow aromatic oil obtained from a tropical Asian grass
with bluish-green lemon-scented leaves. Unfortunately users tended to end
up with yellow coloured skin if they used too much of the stuff!

During the Second World War sprays were successfully developed
for use against mosquitoes and when peace broke out these were put into
action against the midge. Volunteers from forests at Achnashellach and Fort
Augustus in the North-West Highlands assisted in field trials and as a result
the first modern insect repellents were introduced to the timber industry.

A paper by two eminent experts, published in the journal of the
Royal Scottish Forestry Society and entitled "Biting Midges in Scottish
Forestry: A Costly Irritant or a Trivial Nuisance?" reported findings from 14
forest districts as well as data from internal Forestry Commission enquiries.

Some forest managers thought the midge problem affected "only the
weaker among the workforce" but "others from neighbouring districts provided graphic accounts of afflicted work squads."

Worst affected areas were Kintyre, Lochaber and Wester Ross
where at times working conditions became intolerable during the summer
season and operations had to stop completely for several hours at a time on
up to 10 occasions. It also emerged that the higher the level of rainfall, the

worse the incidents of attack.

The experts also reported that certain duties appear to be particularly subject to disruption from midge attacks. These were tasks where the operator required to use both hands. Helmets and visors, worn as protection, tended to attract midges "possibly from the odour of sweat from poorly ventilated headwear."

Although exhaust fumes from chainsaws may deter attacks, at least temporarily, vivid accounts of resumed assaults during re-fuelling were provided by several managers.

In their conclusion the experts state: "Biting midges appear to make an economically significant impact on forestry operations in the western parts of Scotland, in areas associated with high rainfall. The precise cost in productivity is not assessed here but in the extreme west would involve up to 10 days of work disruption and a further 10 days of impaired performance in a range of defined operations. Over the 65 working days of summer this is significant."

They point out that without the range of repellents provided over the past five decades by the Forestry Commission costs to the industry would have been even greater. But as no full and proper field trials have been conducted in Scotland there is little convincing evidence that the current selection of repellents is necessarily the best available.

The experts round off their conclusion by declaring: "A more immediately available solution to the midge problem in Scotland lies in recognising where the midge-induced disruption occurs and when it arises. Although the western sea-board of Scotland has several advantages for forestry, it also has a 65 working day summer period which is subject to regular and largely predictable disruption by biting midges.

"A management response to restrict certain midge-prone operations to the nine-month long midge-free season may be practical in certain work areas. While hand weeding has to be done in summer and felling all the year round, there may be scope for avoiding other midge-prone operations during the summer, at least in the worst affected western areas.

"If this option is available it may prove to make sound commercial sense as well as being the least expensive way of tackling the biting midge.

"Longer term solutions must depend on research into repellents and other forms of personal protection, based on effectively designed field-trials conducted under modern-day criteria.

"THERE IS NO REASON TO ACCEPT THAT THE MIDGE PROBLEM IS UNSOLVABLE."

Farewell my sweet repellent love!

by Gwyneth Mitchell

Midges have been responsible for ruining many a romantic interlude.
Just think, a loving caress on the park bench or the usual quick cuddle at the garden gate can all be wrecked by those little pests that get up your nostrils, in your eyes, and nip furiously at any place where there's a bit of bare flesh. Should a lover's hand wander a little further than it should, in Scotland, you can be assured, the demon midge will be there!

I had all this in mind when back in my teens I set out to meet a swain on a balmy Scottish summer's night. This particular fellow had been a bit of a bone of contention between me and my folks. His style of dress, hair, and swaggering walk did not quite meet with their approval. For a few short weeks I thought he was wonderful. I even hitchhiked eight miles to meet him, and so that the midges would not ruin my appearance, I carefully covered myself with midge repellent. It worked a treat (or so I thought!)

I met the gallant lover outside his boarding house and went to the pub with him for a drink. As it was such a nice evening we decided to take a walk along the harbour. It was perfect. The setting sun had left a deep burnt orange glow along the horizon which blended with the purples and blues of the Northern night sky. The sea was calm except for the ever so gentle lapping of water against the sides of the fishing boats.

My young blade decided it was time to make a move. He aimed surreptitiously for a bite on the back of my neck. So smooth was the movement that I did not know he was there till I heard, "Oh, phew, yuck", splutter, splutter.

What, I wondered, had happened? Had he swallowed a fly?

"That perfume you're wearing has got a terrible taste. Ooh, oh, I'm going to be sick!"

The retchings that followed dispelled all thought of romance and the evening ended with me trying to wipe his face with a tissue and leaving him to recover back at his lodgings.

It seems that it's not only midges that some repellents keep away, they can be satisfactory deterrents for predatory males too! So ladies, be warned, or on the other hand, use the information as a useful tip!

Let us spray

by Denis R. Muir

The cause of this world's present plight?
Nature's interfered with — right?
The answer's with a wee black mite
     at war with man.
It's that, and that alone that spoils
     God's wondrous plan.

Man thinks he's boss — quite wrongly so,
But retaliates against his foe.
Anything that bites must go,
     he attacks with cream
Which makes the fearsome midgie worse
     or so it seems.

To make the cream — man kills the whale
Or murders monkeys if that fails.
Production can't keep up with sales
     of Jungle Gel,
And still the 'Curse of Scotland' bites,
     and bites like hell.

So man responds another way
With chemicals and deadly sprays,
And wonders why the sun's hot rays
     dry up the land.
Meanwhile the midgie population soars
     — they think it's grand.

The End

Other Scottish bestsellers from Lang Syne

Scottish Proverbs

A choice distillation of Scots wit
and wisdom. Gie your tongue mair
holidays than your heid... gie a
beggar a bed, and he'll pay you wi'
a louse... the lass that has mony
wooers aften wails the warst.

ISBN 0-946264-08-2

£4.99

Nessie's Monster Activity Book

Join Nessie, the Loch Ness
Monster, and her friends Sammy
the salmon, Cyril the sheep and
Professor Rufus T. Hamburger,
for hours of activity fun!

ISBN 1-85217-088-3

£2.99

LangSyne
PUBLISHING
WRITING *to* REMEMBER

Other Scottish bestsellers from Lang Syne

Strange old Scots customs and superstitions

Our ancestors were savages who painted their faces, believed in magic and offered human sacrifices to their gods. Some of their ancient customs have survived to the present day while others, thankfully, have passed into history.

ISBN 0-946264-05-8
£4.99

Prophecies of the Brahan Seer

The many strange and amazing things foreseen by Kenneth Mackenzie – famous throughout the Highlands and beyond as the Brahan Seer. Predictions in his day which would have been beyond even the greatest of imaginations have come true centuries later.

ISBN 1-85217-136-7
£5.99

Lang**Syne**

PUBLISHING

WRITING *to* REMEMBER